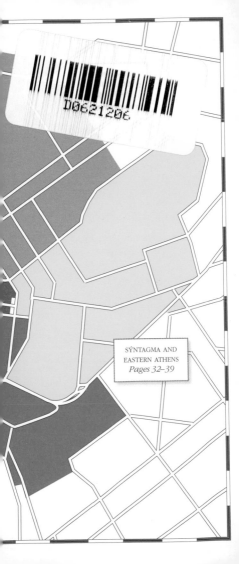

SÝNTAGMA AND
EASTERN ATHENS
Pages 32–39

EYEWITNESS TRAVEL

ATHENS

POCKET GUIDE

DK

LONDON, NEW YORK,
MELBOURNE, MUNICH AND DELHI
www.dk.com

Concept created by Redback Publishing
www.redbackpublishing.com

PACKAGED BY
HourGlass Media
www.hourglassmedia.co.uk

REPRODUCED BY
Colourscan (Singapore)

PRINTED AND BOUND
in China by Leo Paper Products Ltd.

First published in Great Britain in 2010
by Dorling Kindersley Limited, 80 Strand, London WC2R 0RL

Copyright 2010 © Dorling Kindersley Limited, London
A Penguin Company

A CIP CATALOGUE RECORD IS AVAILABLE FROM THE BRITISH LIBRARY.

ISBN 978-1-40534-685-6

We're trying to be cleaner and greener:

- we recycle waste and switch things off
- we use paper from responsibly managed forests whenever possible
- we ask our printers to actively reduce water and energy consumption
- we check out our suppliers' working conditions – they never use child labour

Find out more about our values and best practices at www.dk.com

**The information in this
DK Eyewitness Travel Guide is checked regularly.**
Every effort has been made to ensure that this book is as up-to-date as
possible at the time of going to press. Some details, however, such as
telephone numbers, opening hours, prices, gallery hanging
arrangements and travel information, are liable to change. The
publishers cannot accept responsibility for any consequences arising
from the use of this book, nor for any material on third-party websites,
and cannot guarantee that any website address in this book will be a
suitable source of travel information. We value the views and
suggestions of our readers very highly. Please write to:
Publisher, DK Eyewitness Travel Guides,
Dorling Kindersley, 80 Strand, London WC2R 0RL.

CONTENTS

INTRODUCING ATHENS

ATHENS AREA BY AREA

Hellenistic bronze statue, National Archaeological Museum

Gold cup, Benáki Museum

PRACTICAL INFORMATION

The Temple of Olympian Zeus

Central Athens

Athens has been inhabited for 7,000 years. Its wealth of ancient sites lie within a historic core surrounded by a modern, bustling city. This book divides the city into the four central areas shown below, while two further sections look at the major sights that lie beyond Athens.

Parthenon
One of the most famous buildings in the world, this temple stands as a testament to Athens' fine past (see pp12–13).

Benáki Museum
A first-rate collection of Greek art from Neolithic to present times, housed in a beautifully renovated Neo-Classical mansion with a rooftop view (see p35).

Ancient Agora
Athens' ancient marketplace, founded in the 6th century BC, formed the political heart of the city (see pp28–9).

(see pp28–9)

KEY

M	Metro
	Trolleybus stop
	Funicular
i	Tourist information

DIOU TOU AREOS

ROS ALEXANDRAS

ZAIMI · PEDIOU TRIKOUPI

KALLIDROMIOU

OS IRAKLEIOU

ERESSOU

STREFI HILL

PLATEIA XARCHEIA

TENAKI ANDREA METAXA

ARACHOVIS

TRIKOUPI

MAVROMICHALI

IPPOKRATOUS

ASKLIPIOU

NAVARINOU

CHERN ATHENS

ZALOKOSTA MASSALIAS SINA

SKOUFA

LYKAVITTOS HILL

KONIARI

VALAORITOU

KANARI VOUKOURESTIOU

OMIROU

PLATEIA LYKAVITTOU

PLATEIA KITSIKI NIKOLAO

PLATEIA DANTE

DEINOKRATOUS

IOANNOU GENNADIOU

AMERIKIS

SOLONOS PINDAROU

PLATEIA DEXAMENI

PATRIARCHOU IOAKEIM

SYNTAGMA AND EASTERN ATHENS

KANARI

PLATEIA KOLONAKI

KARNEADOU

LARNEADOU

Evangelismos M

i

ELEFTHERIOU VENIZELOU (V SOFIAS)

Syntagma

LYKEIOU

PLOUTARCHOU

RIZARI

VASILEOS KONSTANTINOU

OTHONOS

LEOFOROS V GEORGIOU B

PATTINOU

IRODOU

LEOFOROS

VASILEOS GEORGIOU B

KALLIRROIS

NATIONAL GARDENS

HELLINON

DE VASILISSIS OLGAS

ARDITTOU

PLATEIA STADIOU

LOFOS ARDITTOU

PLATEIA PLASTIRA

Archimidous

DIAKOU ANAPAFSEOS

KREPATSOU

FIRST CEMETERY OF ATHENS

0 metres 500

0 yards 500

Panagia Gorgoepíkoös
Small in size but not in importance, this 12th-century Byzantine church was built on the site of an ancient temple (see p18).

(see p18)

Athens Highlights

Athens is known as the Classical, marble-pillared cradle of Western civilization. In this kaleidoscopic city, the influences of East and West entwine in the markets, cafés and tavernas, built upon ancient ruins and sitting alongside churches and museums.

Ancient Sites

Acropolis

If you're only in Athens for a day, this is the one sight to see. This is the jewel of Greece, if not the whole of Europe. Its statuesque temples are the most influential buildings in Western architecture (see pp10–11).

Ancient Agora

Socrates, Aristotle and St Paul all held forth at the marketplace below the Acropolis. This was the heart of the ancient city and it is now a great place to wander, imagining the bustle that once filled this historic centre (see pp28–9).

Temple of Olympian Zeus

This colossal temple dedicated to Zeus took nearly 700 years to build. To thank Roman Emperor Hadrian for finally finishing the temple, the Athenians built him an arch (see p20).

Tower of the Winds

Built in 50 BC, there is no other building like it in the ancient world. This eight-sided marble tower housed an ingenious water clock and weather vane (see p16).

Museums and Galleries

National Archaeological Museum

National Archaeological Museum

More than just the best museum in Greece, this is one of the most important museums in the world. It includes finds from some of civilization's greatest cultures (see pp44–5).

New Acropolis Museum

This multi-storey, all-glass museum is a fitting new home for the famous marble sculptures of the Acropolis (see p14).

Museum of Cycladic Art

The world's finest collection of Cycladic art showcases

Hadrian's Arch, next to the Temple of Olympian Zeus

an island culture whose 5,000-year-old figurines still inspire artists of the modern world *(see p36)*.

Benáki Museum

This vast and impressive collection gives a panoramic view of Greek history from the Stone Age (7000 BC) to the present day *(see p35)*. It also has a superb gift shop and rooftop garden restaurant.

Churches and Cathedrals

Panagía Gorgoepikoös

Overshadowed by its huge neighbour, Mitrópoli, this 12th-century church is built of Roman and Byzantine marble relics *(see p18)*.

Mitrópoli

Athens' vast cathedral is one of the city's best-known landmarks. Built in 1862, it is the spiritual centre of the Greek Orthodox Church *(see p17)*.

Agios Nikólaos Ragavás

Typical of 11th-century Byzantine religious architecture, this is a popular location for weddings *(see p16)*.

Kapnikaréa

Surrounded by modern buildings and garment shops, this church is

The 11th-century church of Kapnikaréa

dedicated to the Virgin Mary and decorated with medieval mosaics *(see p24)*.

Green Spaces

National Gardens

The winding paths of the huge, shady National Gardens are a great place to stroll and an unexpected refuge in parched central Athens. There is also a small zoo, a duck pond and a playground *(see p34)*.

The Botanical Museum inside the National Gardens

Pediou Tou Areos

Athens' largest park is a good retreat on blistering city days. Older people crowd the benches while children play soccer around the statues *(see p47)*.

Stréfi Hill

The park of Stréfi Hill is planted with eucalyptus, pines and Mediterranean shrubs, and is criss-crossed by a maze of paths. Climb to the top for a great view of the area *(see p46)*.

Kerameikós

Classical Athens' cemetery contains a fascinating cross-section of life and death, with tombs, temples, sacred roads and an ancient brothel *(see p26)*.

PLÁKA AND SOUTHERN ATHENS

Southern Athens is dominated by the Acropolis and is home to the buildings that were at the heart of ancient Athens. Pláka is one of the oldest inhabited areas of the city. There are many churches and museums to visit and its winding alleyways are full of tavernas and antiques shops.

SIGHTS AT A GLANCE

SEE ALSO

• *Street Life p21*

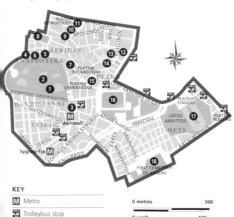

KEY

M Metro

Trolleybus stop

| 0 metres | 500 |
| 0 yards | 500 |

◀ *Busy cafés and tavernas line the narrow streets of Pláka*

Acropolis ❶

Most Greek cities had an acropolis (a hilltop citadel), but this is The Acropolis containing the most important monuments in the Western world. Among them are three temples built to honour the goddess Athena.

The Erechtheion *is situated on the most sacred site of the Acropolis. This temple was built as a sanctuary to both the goddess Athena Polias and the god Erechtheus-Poseidon.*

The Propylaia *was built in 437–432 BC to form a new entrance to the Acropolis.*

The Temple of Athena Nike *was built in 426–421 BC to commemorate the Athenians' victories over the Persians.*

The Beulé Gate *was the first entrance to the Acropolis.*

Pathway to Acropolis from ticket office

The Theatre of Herodes Atticus, *also known as the Odeion of Herodes Atticus, was originally built in AD 161. It was restored in 1955 and is used today for outdoor concerts.*

The Parthenon *is one of the world's most famous buildings. Although few sculptures are left on this temple, some can still be admired, such as this one from the east pediment (see pp12–13).*

VISITORS' CHECKLIST

Map C5. Dionysíou Areopagítou. Tel 210 321 0219. Open daily (times vary) except 1 Jan, 25 Mar, Easter Sun, 1 May, 25, 26 Dec. Summer adm charge (free Sun). **www.culture.gr**

Old Acropolis Museum

Two Corinthian columns *are all that remain of the monuments erected to display the trophies from theatrical contests.*

Shrine of Asklepios

The Acropolis rock *was an easily defended site. It has been in use for nearly 5,000 years.*

The Theatre of Dionysos *was built in 342–326 BC and seated 15,000. The figure of the comic satyr, Silenus, can be seen here.*

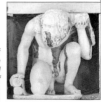

Parthenon ❷

This temple was designed to house a statue of the goddess Athena Parthenos (Maiden) that was 12 m (40 ft) high. It took nine years to complete and was dedicated to the goddess in 438 BC. Over the centuries, it has been used as a church, a mosque and an arsenal, and has suffered severe damage.

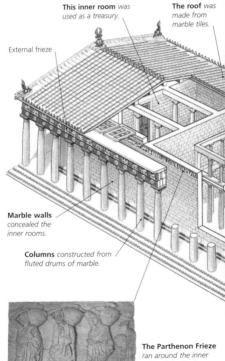

This inner room was used as a treasury.

The roof was made from marble tiles.

External frieze

Marble walls concealed the inner rooms.

Columns constructed from fluted drums of marble.

The Parthenon Frieze ran around the inner walls of the Parthenon. It depicted the Great Panathenaia festival, honouring the goddess Athena.

The Parthenon
*was the epitome
of ancient Greek
Classical art, a
magnificent temple
to the virgin goddess
Athena. It remains
the city's emblem
today.*

The northeast corner
*shows the remains of the
pediment sculptures.*

The internal columns
*were in two rows and
Doric in style.*

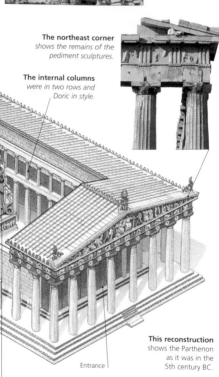

This reconstruction
*shows the Parthenon
as it was in the
5th century BC.*

Entrance

The Statue of Athena, *vast in size and made out of
ivory and gold, was the focus of the Parthenon. No trace
of it remains today but a smaller Roman copy can be seen
in the National Archaeological Museum (see pp44–5).*

The entrance to the New Acropolis Museum

New Acropolis Museum ❸

Map C6. Makrigiánni 2–4. Adm charge. For opening times, go to www.newacropolismuseum.gr.

Lying at the foot of the Acropolis, this new €130-million, multi-storey, glass, showpiece museum, designed by architect Bernard Tschumi, is undoubtedly a fitting home for the stunning treasures it contains. Tschumi had the added challenge of constructing the building over the excavations of a Christian settlement. Concrete pillars and a glass walkway allow the building to hover over the ruins, which are on view in the lobby near the entrance. The rest of the collection is in chronological order.

The Archaic Collection is set out in a magnificent gallery. Fragments of pedimental statues include mythological scenes of Herakles grappling with various monsters and the more peaceful votive

The Calf-Bearer

statue of the *Moschophoros*, or Calf-Bearer, portraying a young man carrying a calf on his shoulders from around 570 BC.

The sky-lit Parthenon Gallery on the top floor is the highlight. Here, arranged around an indoor court and looking out onto the Parthenon, the remaining parts of the Parthenon frieze are displayed in the order in which they would have graced the Parthenon (there are blank spaces left for those held in London). The sculptures depict the Panathenaic procession, including the chariot and *apobates* (slaves riding chariot horses) and a sacrificial cow being led by youths.

On the level below, the post-Parthenon Collection comprises sculptures from the Temple of Athena Nike, and architectural features from the Propylaia and the Erechtheion, including four caryatids from the south porch.

Kanellópoulos Museum ❹

Map C5. Corner of Theorías and Pános 12. Open Tues–Sun except 1 Jan, 25 Mar, Easter Sun, 25, 26 Dec. Adm charge.

This museum contains a varied collection of artifacts from all over the Hellenistic world, including 6th-century BC helmets, 5th-century BC gold Persian jewellery and Attic vases. A huge stone block that fell from the walls of the Acropolis was so heavy that the museum was built around it. It can still be seen on the ground floor.

University of Athens Museum ❺

Map C5. Thólou 5. Open Mon–Fri except public hols. Free.

This was the first home of the University of Athens. It opened in 1837 but in 1841 the University moved to its new quarters. In 1963, the building was declared a National Monument. Later reacquired by the university, the old building was opened as a museum in 1974. Today, it has an eclectic collection of memorabilia such as anatomical models and scientific instruments.

Old medical artifacts at the University of Athens Museum

Anafiótika ❻

Map C5.

Clinging to the side of the Acropolis is Athens' loveliest and quirkiest hidden neighbourhood. It was built in the 19th century by tradesmen from the Cycladic island of Anafi, brought to Athens after the War of Independence to build King Otto's palace. They missed home so much that they decided to re-create a pocket of it here with island-style, dome-topped blue-and-white houses in a maze of tiny passageways. Many descendents of the original Anafi workers still live here. The area is bounded by two 17th-century churches: Agios Geórgios tou Vráchou to the east and Agios Symeón to the west.

Terracotta sphinxes on a roof in Anafiótika

Site of the marble-pillared Roman Forum

Agios Nikólaos Ragavás 7

Map C5. Corner of Prytaneiou & Epichármou. Open daily. Free.

This is a typical 11th-century Byzantine church. It was rebuilt in the 18th century and restored to some of its former glory in the late 1970s. It is one of the favourite parish churches of Pláka and is used for colourful Greek weddings that often spill out onto the street. It was the first church in Athens to have a bell after the War of Independence (1821), and the first to ring out after the city's liberation from the Germans on 12 October 1944.

Agios Nikólaos Ragavás

Roman Forum and Tower of the Winds 8

Map C5. Within Roman Agora ruins. Open daily except public holidays. Adm charge.

In the 1st century AD, the Romans moved Athens' marketplace here from the old Agora. Smaller than the original, this marble-pillared courtyard became the administrative and commercial centre of the city until the 19th century. Its showpiece was the Tower of the Winds built by Syrian astronomer Andrónikos Kyrrestes in 50 BC. This octagonal marble tower was built as a combined weather vane and water clock and has the personification of the winds on each side.

Museum of Greek Popular Musical Instruments 9

Map C5. Diogénous 1–3. Open Tue–Sun except 17 Nov and public hols. Free.

Cretan musicologist Phoebus Anogianákis donated more than 1,200 musical instruments from his impressive collection to the Greek State in 1978. In 1991 this museum was opened, devoted to the history of popular Greek music. Instruments from all over Greece are displayed including Byzantine lyres, ivory lutes and gypsy flutes, with recordings and headphones at every exhibit. It is also an ethnomusicology study centre, and occasional performances are held in the courtyard.

Traditional Greek lute

Panagía Gorgoepikoös ⑩

See p18.

Mitrópoli ⑪

Map D5. Plateía Mitropóleos. Open daily. Free.

Athens' massive cathedral was finished in 1862. It had taken 20 years to complete, involved three architects and used marble from 72 demolished churches for its walls. It was the first major church to be built after Greece's independence in 1821 and it became the seat of the Bishop of Athens. Though its colourful frescoes and ecclesiastical objects are impressive, its architecture is considerably less so. Mitrópoli's importance is almost entirely spiritual, as the central point of the Greek Orthodox Church.

Russian Church of the Holy Trinity ⑫

Map D5. Filellínon 21. Open daily except public hols. Free.

Still in use by the Russian community, this was once the largest church in the city. Built in 1031, it was ruined by an earthquake in 1701 and restored in 1847 by the Russian government. A large cruciform building, its most unusual feature is its wide dome. Its interior was decorated by the Bavarian painter Ludwig Thiersch. The bell tower dates from the 19th century, its bell a gift from Tsar Alexander II.

The entrance to Athens' cathedral, Mitrópoli

Panagía Gorgoepíkoös ❿

This domed cruciform church was built in the 12th century entirely from marble. Its diminutive size was suitable for Athens, which was just a village at the time. Adorned with friezes and bas-reliefs, the exterior mixes Classical and Byzantine styles.

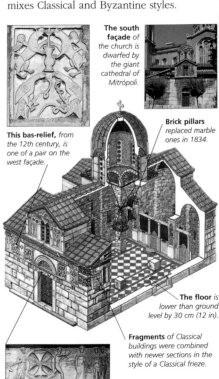

The south façade of the church is dwarfed by the giant cathedral of Mitrópoli.

This bas-relief, from the 12th century, is one of a pair on the west façade.

Brick pillars replaced marble ones in 1834.

The floor is lower than ground level by 30 cm (12 in).

Fragments of Classical buildings were combined with newer sections in the style of a Classical frieze.

The lintel frieze, depicting the months of the year, dates from the 4th century BC. The central cross was added in the 12th century.

VISITORS' CHECKLIST

Map D5. Plateía Mitropóleos. Open daily. Free.

Reconstruction of the Pátra synagogue's ark, Jewish Museum

Jewish Museum of Greece **⑬**

Map D5. Níkis 39. Open Mon–Fri, Sun (times vary) except public hols and Jewish festivals. Adm charge.

This small museum traces the history of Greece's Jewish communities, which date back to the 3rd century BC. The 15,000 items on display in a series of rooms present a revealing portrait of the Sephardic Jews who fled Spain and Portugal in the 15th century to settle throughout Greece in the religiously tolerant years of the Ottoman Empire. There are also displays that record the German occupation of Greece during World War II.

Museum of Greek Folk Art **⑭**

Map D5. Kydathinaíon 17. Open Tue–Sun except public hols. Adm charge.

This dimly lit government-run building houses an impressive collection of Greek folk art from 1650 to the present day, displayed on five floors. Exhibits include costumes, ceramics, puppets

tapestries, filigree jewellery and embroidery. The decorative crafts displayed here reveal a rich heritage of traditional techniques in skills such as weaving, woodcarving and metal-work. Not to be missed is the room full of frescoes by internationally renowned folk artist Theófilos Chatzimichaïl, transported from his home on Lésvos.

One of the exhibits at the Museum of Greek Folk Art

Plateía Lysikrátous **⑮**

Map D5. Lysikrátous, Sélley & Epimenídou.

This square is named after the monument of Lysikrates that dominates it. Built in 334 BC, this is the city's only intact choregic monument. These monuments were built to commemorate the victors at the annual choral and dramatic festival at the Theatre of Dionysos *(see*

The monument of Lysikrates

p11). They take their name from the rich sponsor *(choregos)* who produced the winning team. Not far from this is the 11th-century Byzantine church of Agía Aikateríni (St Catherine). Once part of the monastery of St Catherine, in 1882 it became a parish church.

A fallen column at the site of the Temple of Olympian Zeus

Temple of Olympian Zeus ⑯

Map D6. Corner of Amalias and Vassilissis Olgas. Open daily except public hols. Adm charge (free Sun, Nov–Mar).

The Temple of Olympian Zeus is the largest temple in mainland Greece, exceeding even the Parthenon (*see pp12–13*) in size. Zeus had long been worshipped on this site, and there was at least one other temple to him before this one.

Work began on this vast edifice in the 6th century BC, in the reign of the tyrant Peisistratos, who allegedly initiated the building work to gain public favour. Political turmoil delayed its completion, and it was not finished until 650 years later.

The Roman Emperor Hadrian dedicated the temple to Zeus Olympios during the Panhellenic festival of AD 132, on his second visit to Athens. He also set up a gold and ivory inlaid statue of the god inside the temple. Next to it he placed a huge statue of himself. Both these statues have since been lost.

Only 15 of the original 104 Corinthian columns remain, each 17 m (56 ft) high – but enough to give a sense of the enormous size of this temple, which would have been approximately 96 m (315 ft) long and 40 m (130 ft) wide. Corinthian capitals were added to the simple Doric columns by a Roman architect in 174 BC.

To thank Hadrian for finishing the temple, the Athenians built a two-storey arch next to the temple in AD 131. It was positioned to mark the boundary between the ancient city of Theseus and Hadrian's new Athens.

The remaining Corinthian columns dedicated to Zeus Olympios

Kallimármaro Stadium ⑰

Map E6. Archimídous 16. Open daily. Free.

This huge marble stadium occupies the exact site of the original 4th-century BC Panathenaic Stadium, rebuilt in white marble for the Panathenaic Games in AD 144. It was restored as a faithful replica for the first modern Olympics in 1896.

The vast Kallimármaro Stadium

First Cemetery of Athens ⑱

Map E7. Entrance in Anapáfseos. Open daily. Free.

Athens' municipal cemetery is a peaceful place planted with cypress trees. Fine examples of 19th-century funerary art can be seen here. In addition to the tombs of famous people, such as the actress and politician Melína Merkoúri and archaeologist Heinrich Schliemann, the cemetery also contains a moving memorial to the 40,000 Athenians who perished through starvation during World War II.

STREET LIFE

RESTAURANTS

O Platanos
Map C5. Diogénous 4.
Tel 210 322 0666.
Cheap
Taverna founded in 1932 with exceptionally good retsina.

Tzitzikas and Mermigas
Map D5. Mitropóleos 12–14.
Tel 210 324 7607.
Moderate
Modern Greek taverna with some vegetarian dishes.

Daphne's
Map D6. Lysikrátous 4.
Tel 210 322 7971.
Expensive
Greek gourmet cuisine in a Neo-Classical building.

BARS AND CAFÉS

Klepsydra
Map C5. Thrasyvoúlou.
Tiny, quiet bar-café.

See p80 for price codes.

To Tistrato
Map D5. Aggelou Geronta and Daidalou.
Spectacular pastries in old-world atmosphere.

Dioskouri
Map C5. Dioskoúdon 9.
Hidden ouzeri popular with students. Good to visit for sunset drink and appetizers.

SHOPPING

Lalaounis Museum Jewellery Shop
Map C6. Corner of Karyatidon and Kallisperi.
Glamorous gold creations.

Mesogeia
Map D5. Nikis 52 & Kydathinaion.
Little gem of a grocery shop with fine Greek produce.

Emblem
Map D6. Makrigianni 15c.
Good for souvenirs and gifts.

MONASTIRÁKI AND WESTERN ATHENS

The once-neglected old neighbourhoods that make up this area have now been transformed into some of the hippest places in the city. Here, ancient Roman and Ottoman sites nestle next to a lively mix of market stalls, bars and clubs, and squares filled with outdoor cafés and restaurants.

SIGHTS AT A GLANCE

Ancient Sites
Ancient Agora
pp28–9 **12**
Kerameikós **9**

Churches and Cathedrals
First Synagogue of Athens **6**
Kapnikaréa **1**
Pantanassa Church **4**

Historical Buildings
Hadrian's Library **2**

Markets
Flea Market **5**

Museums and Galleries
Agora Museum **13**
Athinais/Museum of
  Diachronic Art **15**
Benáki Islamic Art
  Museum **7**
Folk Ceramic Museum **3**
Kerameikós Museum **10**
Municipal Art Gallery **8**
Technopolis **11**

Parks and Gardens
Filopáppos Hill **14**

SEE ALSO

• Street Life p31

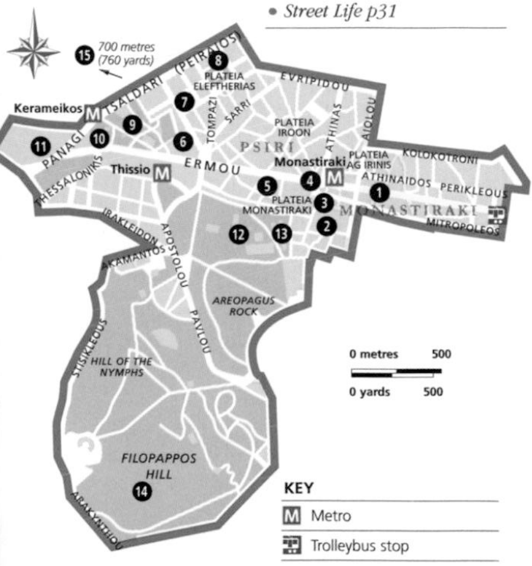

KEY

| Ⓜ | Metro |
| 🚏 | Trolleybus stop |

◀ Shoppers in Adrianoú at the centre of Monastiráki flea market

Some of the surviving walls and columns of Hadrian's Library

Hadrian's Library ❶

Map C5. Entrance on Areos. Open daily. Adm charge.

Roman Emperor Hadrian built this library in AD 131. It had a marble courtyard, mosaic floors, concert areas and a place for storing library scrolls. Following an extensive restoration project, part of the site is now open.

Kapnikaréa ❷

Map C4. Corner of Ermoú and Kalamiótou. Open Sun–Fri (times vary) except public hols. Free.

Dating from the 11th century, this Byzantine church was rescued from demolition in 1834. It is now surrounded by office blocks

The dome and main entrance of the Byzantine Kapnikaréa

and shops. Traditionally called the Church of the Princess, its foundation is attributed to Empress Irene, who ruled the Byzantine Empire from AD 797 to 802. Restored in the 1950s, the dome of the church is supported by four Roman columns. Frescoes by Fótis Kóntoglou (1885–1965) were painted during the restoration project.

Folk Ceramic Museum ❸

Map C4. Tzistarákis Mosque, Areos 1. Open Mon & Wed–Sun except public hols. Adm charge.

This outpost of the Museum of Greek Folk Art is housed in the imposing Tzistarákis Mosque, also known as the Mosque of the Lower Fountain. The extensive collection includes rich, colourful ceramics, beautiful sculptures and decorative objects from all over Greece and Asia Minor. Most of the exhibits are made from terracotta or the gleaming faïence that was favoured by the ancient Minoans. The collection was donated by Professor Vasíleios Kyriazópoulos in 1974. The mosque was built in 1759 by the Turkish civil governor and restored after earthquake damage in 1981.

Pantanassa Church ④

Map C4. Plateía Monastirakíou. Open daily. Free.

Situated on Monastiráki Square, this tiny Byzantine church was built in the 11th century. Originally, Pantanassa Church belonged to the monastery (*monastirí*) that gave the area its name. Alterations were made in the 17th century and the bell tower was added in 1911.

Dome of the 11th-century Pantanassa Church

Flea Market ⑤

Map C4. From Plateía Avyssinías to Plateía Monastirakíou. Open Sunday.

On Sunday mornings, this sprawling and varied market bursts into life as traders set out their bric-a-brac stalls. Here you can find everything from ancient coins to fake designer sunglasses. For the locals, the heart of this market lies in Plateía Avyssinías and its surrounding streets. It is advisable to arrive before 11am as most of the good things disappear quickly and the streets become crowded.

First Synagogue of Athens ⑥

Map B4. Melidoni 8. Open on request.

Before World War II, this area was the centre of Athens' thriving Jewish community. Built in 1904, this is the oldest synagogue in Athens. Across the street, the Beth-Salom Synagogue is now Athens' main community synagogue.

Benáki Islamic Art Museum ⑦

Map B4. Agion Asomaton 22 & Dipilou 12. Open Tue–Sun except public hols (free Wed). Adm charge

In a smart Neo-Classical building, this museum was founded in 1931 by Antónis Benákis (1873–1954) to display Islamic ceramics, jewellery, metalwork and woodwork from the 7th to the 19th centuries. It is one of the most important collections in the world. There is also a rooftop café that overlooks the cemetery of Kerameikós (*see p26*).

Bric-a-brac on sale in the Flea Market

Miss T K, by Giánnis Mitarákis, in the Municipal Art Gallery

Municipal Art Gallery ⑧

Map B3. Pireos 51, Plateía Koumoundoúrou. Open daily (times vary) except 3 Oct and public hols. Free.

This little-visited museum has one of the finest archive collections of modern Greek art. Designed in 1872, the home of the museum is the old Foundling Hospital. It was built to cope with the city's population explosion towards the end of the 19th century; unwanted babies were left outside the main entrance to be cared for by hospital staff.

The Municipality of Athens has been amassing the collection since 1923. It now offers an excellent introduction to the diverse styles of modern Greek artists. Many paintings are passionate reflections on the Greek landscape, such as Dímos Mpraésas' (1878–1967) landscapes of the Cyclades. Paintings such as Nikólaos Kartsonákis' *Street Market* (1939) also reveal the folk roots that are at the heart of much modern Greek art.

Kerameikós ⑨

Map B4. Ermoú 148. Open daily (times vary). Adm charge.

This ancient cemetery has been a burial ground since the 12th century BC. Heroes and statesmen were buried beneath the tombs lining the roads. It was also the scene of far shadier activities: the haunt of prostitutes, money-lenders and wine-sellers.

Most of the monuments remaining today date from the 4th century BC and can be seen along the Street of the Tombs. The different styles, from the lavish relief sculptures to the simple small columns, all reveal the dignity typical of Greek funerary art. The sculptures were excavated in the early 1900s and the originals are now in the National Archaeological Museum (*see pp44–5*) and the Kerameikós Museum (*see p27*); however, plaster copies of the originals can be seen *in situ*.

The high, round burial mounds lining the holy road date from the 7th century BC and were probably first built to honour great warriors.

This relief, the Stele of Dexileos, marks the grave of a young warrior

Kerameikós Museum ⑩

Map A4. Ermoú 148. Open daily (times vary). Adm charge.

This small museum contains fine examples of Greek urns and other pottery ornaments as well as the originals of many tombs found at the ancient cemetery of Kerameikós. The museum was built in the 1930s with donations made by German-American industrialist Gustav Oberlander (1867–1936). The most moving exhibits here come from the children's graves and include pottery toy horses and terracotta dolls.

Oberlander Museum amphora

Technopolis ⑪

Map A4. Peiraiós 100. Open daily. Free.

Based in the old city gasworks, this vast multi-purpose arts complex opened in 1999. It was instrumental in initiating the urban regeneration of Gazi, once a run-down industrial zone but now Athens' hippest nightlife district. At Technopolis, which means art city, the defunct gasometers, brick outbuildings and spacious courtyard now host exhibitions, concerts and a bar-restaurant. The towering brick chimneys are lit red at night as a symbol of new art in an urban environment.

Ancient Agora ⑫

See pp28–9.

Agora Museum ⑬

Map C5. Main entrance at Adriánou. Open daily (times vary) except public hols. Adm charge.

The Stoa of Attalos originally served as a 2nd-century BC shopping mall. Both arcades were divided into shops, and the cool, marble-pillared space was a popular place for wealthy Athenians to meet. It was reconstructed in the 1950s and converted into a museum to display finds from the Ancient Agora. Most of the museum's exhibits are closely connected with the development of democracy in Athens. Outside, in the marble passage, the statues that once adorned the temples in the marketplace are on display.

Colonnades of the reconstructed Stoa of Attalos, now the Agora Museum

Ancient Agora ⑫

The Agora, or marketplace, formed the
political heart of ancient Athens from 600 BC.
Excavations began in the 1930s and, since
then, the vast remains of a complex array of
public buildings have been revealed.

The Agora, as
seen from the
south, showing
the reconstructed
Stoa of Attalos
on the right.

The Stoa of Attalos was
where wealthy Athenians
went to shop and gossip.

Odeion of Agrippa
*This statue of a triton
(half-god, half-fish)
once adorned the
façade of the Odeion
of Agrippa. It dates
from AD 150 and is
now in the Agora
Museum (see p27).*

Temple of Ares

The Panathenaic Way was
named after the Great
Panathenaia festival which
took place every four years.

The ruins of the Nymphaion – a 2nd-century fountainhouse – are still visible, despite the building of a Byzantine church over it in the 11th century.

VISITORS' CHECKLIST

Map B5. Main entrance at Adriánou. Tel 210 321 0185. Open daily (times vary) except 1 Jan, 25 Mar, Easter Sun, 1 May, 25, 26 Dec. Adm charge.

The middle stoa housed shops.

This reconstruction shows the Agora as it was in around AD 200, viewed from the northwest.

The Tholos was the Council headquarters.

Monument of the Eponymous Heroes

Arsenal

Hephaisteion, also called the Theseion, is the best-preserved building on the site. This temple was built around 449–440 BC.

Filopáppos Hill ⑭

Map B6. Entrance off Dionysiou Areopagitou.

The highest summit in the south of Athens, at 147 m (482 ft), offers spectacular views of the Acropolis. In ancient times, Greeks believed Filopáppos Hill was inhabited by the muses of art, music and poetry. The Monument of Philopappus on its summit was built between AD 114 and 116 in honour of Caius Julius Antiochus Philopappus, a Roman consul and philhellene. Its unusual concave marble façade, 12 m (40 ft) high, contains niches with statues of Philopappus and his grandfather, Antiochus IV. A frieze depicts the arrival of Philopappus by chariot for his inauguration as Roman consul in AD 100.

Meeting place of the first citizens' assembly at Pnyx Hill

Pnyx Hill

If Athens is the cradle of democracy, Pnyx Hill is its exact birthplace. During the 4th and 5th century BC the citizens' assembly met here to discuss and vote upon all but the most important matters of state, until it lost its powers during Roman rule. The speaker's platform is still visible today.

Hill of the Nymphs

Believed to be the dwelling place of nymphs, this 103-m (340-ft) high tree-clad hill takes its name from dedications found carved on rocks in today's Observatory Garden. Built in 1842, the Observatory occupies the site of a sanctuary to nymphs associated with childbirth.

Socrates is believed to have been imprisoned in a cave on Filopáppos Hill

Athinais/Museum of Diachronic Art ⑮

Kastorias 34–36, Votanikos–Gazi. 400 m (440 yards) NW of Technopolis (see p27). Open daily.

This converted 1920s silk factory opened as a multipurpose arts centre in 2000. Following alterations in 2008, Athinais now has two museums, a theatre, a music hall and an excellent bar-restaurant. The centre also houses the Museum of Diachronic Art, which exhibits works by contemporary Greek artists and world-famous modern painters and sculptors, while the Museum of Ancient Cypriot Art displays ceramics dating back to the 9th century BC. Smart residential units occupy the adjoining Athinais Tower Lofts.

STREET LIFE

RESTAURANTS

Thanassis
Map D5. Mitropóleos 69.
Tel 210 324 4705.
Cheap
Arguably serves the best souvlaki and yiros in town.

Kouzina
Map B4. Sarri 44.
Tel 210 321 5534.
Moderate
Creative Mediterranean cuisine with adjoining open-air cinema Jun–Sep.

To Kouti
Map D5. Adrianou 23.
Tel 210 321 3229.
Moderate
Great spot for lunch while sightseeing.

Tou Psyrri
Map C4. Aischylou 12.
Tel 210 321 4923.
Moderate
Popular taverna serving traditional favourites.

BARS & CAFÉS

Café Aeolis
Map C4. Aiolou 23.
Trendy cafe for light lunches.

See p80 for price codes.

Café Avissynias
Map C4. Plateía Avissynías.
Belle époque gem offering French and Arab food.

Soul
Map C4. Evripidou 65.
Stylish bar and courtyard garden with Chinese lanterns.

Bar Tesera
Map D4. Kolokotroni 25.
Bar with occasional art exhibitions.

SHOPPING

Aristokratikon
Map D4. Karageorgi Servias 9 (off Athinaidos Perikleous).
Chocolates for connoisseurs freshly handmade every day.

Bahar
Map C4. Evripidou 31.
One of the best-known family-run shops selling herbs.

Centre of Hellenic Tradition
Map D5. Mitropóleos 59.
Handicrafts from every corner of the country.

Katerina
Map C4. Ifaistou 21.
Wooden backgammon boards.

SÝNTAGMA AND EASTERN ATHENS

Plateía Syntágmatos is the centre of modern Athens and home to the Greek Parliament. Nearby, many fine museums can be found alongside the smart district of Kolonáki. This is the place to go for shopping, people-watching and glamorous café-sitting. Above it all lies Lykavittós Hill, with its famous theatre and views.

SIGHTS AT A GLANCE

Historic Areas and Buildings
Gennádeion ⑩
Presidential Palace ③

Squares, Parks and Gardens
Lykavittós Hill ⑪
National Gardens ②
Plateía Kolonakíou ⑨
Plateía Syntágmatos ①

Museums and Galleries
Benáki Museum ④
Byzantine Museum ⑥
Museum of Cycladic Art ⑤
National Gallery of Art ⑧
War Museum ⑦

SEE ALSO

• Street Life p39

KEY

M	Metro
	Trolleybus stop
	Funicular
i	Tourist information

0 metres	500
0 yards	500

◀ The courtyard of the Byzantine Museum, near Sýntagma

The imposing parliament building in Plateía Syntágmatos

Plateía Syntágmatos ❶

Map D4. Sýntagma.

This square (also known as Sýntagma Square) is home to the Greek parliament, housed in the impressive Voulí building. Constructed in 1842 as a palace for King Otto, today it is a single-chamber council for parliament and only its library is open to the public.

Also standing in the square is the Tomb of the Unknown Soldier, unveiled on 25 March 1932 (National Independence Day). The soldiers of the National Guard (*évzones*) are on continuous patrol at the tomb dressed in their traditional uniform of kilt and pompom clogs. They are best seen at the changing of the guard every Sunday at 11am.

Sýntagma metro station is as much a museum as a transport hub. When it was being built, archaeologists found thousands of priceless items on this site. Many are displayed in the station, but the highlight is a glass wall looking directly onto the site with detailed descriptions of its ancient layers.

National Gardens ❷

Map E5. Borders Vasilíssis Sofías, Iródou Attikoú, Vasilíssis Olgas and Vasilíssis Amalías.
Open daily. Free.

Behind the parliament building, this 16-ha (40-acre) park, cherished by all Athenians and formerly known as the "Royal Gardens", was renamed the National Gardens by decree in 1923. Queen Amalía ordered the creation of the park in the 1840s. She used the fledgling Greek Navy to bring 15,000 seedlings from around the world. Although the gardens have lost much of their original grandeur, they remain one of the most peaceful spots in the city.

The tranquil and shady National Gardens of Athens

Shady paths meander past small squares, park benches and ponds filled with goldfish. Remains of Roman mosaics excavated in the park and an old aqueduct add atmosphere. Modern sculptures of writers can be found throughout the park. There is also a small botanical museum to visit, a ramshackle zoo and some cafés.

Presidential Palace 3

Map E5. Iródou Attikoú. Closed to the public.

This former royal palace was designed and built by Neo-Classical architect, Ernst Ziller in around 1878. It was occupied by the Greek Royal Family from 1890 until the hasty departure of King Constantine in 1967. It is still guarded by the *évzones* whose barracks are at the top of the street. After the abolition of the monarchy, it became the official residence of the President of Greece and he still uses it today when hosting dignitaries. Its well-maintained gardens can just be seen through the railings.

Gold band, Benáki Museum

Benáki Museum 4

Map E4. Corner of Koumpári & Vassilísis Sofías. Open Wed–Mon (times vary) except public hols. Adm charge (free Thu).

This outstanding museum was founded in 1931 by Antónis Benákis (1873–1954), the son of Emmanouíl, a wealthy Greek who made his fortune in Egypt. Housed in an elegant Neo-Classical mansion, which was once the home of the Benákis family, the vast collection contains a diverse array of Greek arts and crafts, paintings and jewellery, local costumes and political memorabilia that spans over 5,000 years, from the Neolithic era to the 20th century. There are over 20,000 objects laid out chronologically in 36 rooms.

The white Neo-Classical mansion of the Benáki Museum

The entrance to the elegant Stathátos Mansion

Museum of Cycladic Art ❺

Map F4. Neofýtou Doúka 4, (entrance to Stathátos Mansion at Irodótou 1). Open Wed–Mon (times vary) except public hols. Adm charge.

Opened in 1986, this modern museum displays the world's finest collection of Cycladic art. It was initially assembled by Nikólas and Dolly Goulandrí and has expanded with donations from other Greek collectors. The museum now has an excellent selection of ancient Greek and Cypriot art, the earliest from about 5,000 years ago. The Cycladic figurines, dating from the 3rd millennium BC, have never enjoyed quite the same level of popularity as Classical sculpture. However, the beautiful marble carvings are unlike anything found in contemporary civilizations. Most are female forms –

possibly cult objects of a goddess religion – and their elemental shapes have inspired many 20th-century artists and sculptors, including Picasso, Modigliani and Moore.

Around the Gallery

In the main building, the Cycladic collection is on the first floor, ancient Greek art is on the second and the third shows ancient Cypriot art. The fourth floor houses a permanent exhibition entitled *Scenes from Daily Life in Antiquity*.

Stathátos Mansion

Built in 1895, this stylish Neo-Classical mansion was opened as a wing of the museum in 1992. Temporary exhibitions are displayed here.

The Goulandris Dynasty

The museum's founders, the Goulandris family, are arguably Greece's greatest shipping dynasty (they had a long-standing rivalry with Onassis). They are also known for their legacy in arts: in addition to the Museum of Cycladic Art, the family is planning a new Museum of Modern Art in Athens.

Cycladic figurine

One of a series of Cycladic marble vessels on display in the museum

Byzantine Museum ⑥

Map F5. Vasilissis Sofías 22, Plateía Rigílis. Open Tue–Sun except public hols. Adm charge.

Originally called the Villa Ilissía, this elegant Florentine-style mansion was built between 1840 and 1848 for the Duchesse de Plaisance (1785–1854). This woman was the wife of one of Napoleon's generals, and was a key figure in the city of Athens during the mid-19th century and a dedicated philhellene.

Collector Geórgios Sotiríou converted the house into a museum in the 1930s. The entrance was turned into a monastic court, with a copy of a fountain from a 4th-century mosaic in Dafní *(see pp52–3)*. In summer, concerts are often held in the courtyard.

The museum's collection is divided into two sections. Section one, *From the Ancient World to Byzantine*, traces the rise of Christianity, and is dominated by fragments of stone carvings and mosaics taken from basilicas, sarcophagi and early religious sculpture.

A 14th-century icon of St Michael in the Byzantine Museum

Section two, *The Byzantine World*, runs from the 6th century AD up until the fall of Constantinople in 1453 and presents an array of icons, ecclesiastical artifacts and frescoes.

Aristotle's Lyceum

Building plans for the neighbouring site were shelved when excavators discovered some ancient ruins. These were identified as the Lyceum of Aristotle (the school the philosopher founded to compete with Plato's Academy). The site has been taken over by the Byzantine Museum.

The courtyard of the Byzantine Museum

War Museum ❼

Map F4. Corner of Vasilíssis Sofías and Rizári. Open Tue–Sun except public hols. Free.

The War Museum was opened in 1975 after the fall of the military dictatorship. Galleries contain armour, battle scenes and plans from as far back as Mycenaean times through to the German occupation of 1941. There is a fine display of pictures of leaders from the Greek War of Independence and art that recalls the hardships of the two world wars.

The façade of the War Museum

National Gallery of Art ❽

Map G5. Vasiléos Konstantínou 50. Open Wed–Mon (times vary) except public hols. Adm charge.

Greece's most important art gallery, the National Gallery of Art, was opened in 1976. Housed in a modern low-rise building, it contains a permanent collection of European and Greek art. Masterpieces by El Greco (1541–1614) are the highlight of the collection. The gallery also hosts major travelling exhibitions.

Plateía Kolonakíou ❾

Map E4. Kolonáki.

Kolonáki Square and its neighbouring side streets are the most chic and

People sitting in a lively pavement café in Plateía Kolonakíou

sophisticated part of Athens. The square is named after a small ancient column (*kolonáki*) found in the area. Celebrated for its designer boutiques and fashionable bars and cafés, smart shops and *ouzeri*, it revels in its status as the city's most fashionable quarter.

Gennádeion ❿

Map G4. American School of Classical Studies, Souidias 61. Open Mon–Sat (times vary) except Aug and public hols. Free.

The Greek diplomat and bibliophile Ioánnis Gennádios (1844–1932) spent a lifetime accumulating rare first editions and illuminated manuscripts. In 1923, he donated his

Ionic columns at the front of the imposing Gennádeion building

collection to the American School of Classical Studies. Visitors may look at selected exhibits including poet Edward Lear's sketches.

Lykavittós Hill ⓫

Map F3. Funicular: from Ploutárchou. Open daily (times vary).

Open-air theatre on Lykavittós Hill

The peak of Lykavittós (also known as Lycabettus) reaches 277 m (910 ft) above the city, and is its highest hill. It can be climbed on foot by various paths or by taking a ride in the funicular, which leaves from the

corner of Ploutárchou. On foot it should take about 45 minutes. The hill may derive its name from the words *lyki* and *vaino*, meaning "path of light". The small chapel of Agios Geórgios crowns the top of the hill where there is also a summit restaurant, café and open-air theatre.

STREET LIFE

RESTAURANTS

Il Postino
Map E3. Grivaíon 3, alley off Skoufá. Tel 210 364 1414.
Moderate
Cosy, genuine osteria serving Italian home-cooking.

Altamira
Map E4. Tsakalof 36A.
Tel 210 361 4695.
Moderate
Mexican, Arabian & Asian food.

To Ouzadiko
Map F4. Karneádou 25–29.
Tel 210 729 5484.
Moderate
Busy ouzeri hidden away serving traditional mezes.

Orizontes Lykavittóu
Map F3. Lykavittós Hill.
Tel 210 722 7065.
Expensive
Mediterranean restaurant near the top of Lykavittós Hill.

See p80 for price codes.

BARS

Balthazar
Map E3. Tsoha & Soutsou 27.
Elegant bar in the gardens of a Neo-Classical mansion.

Briki
Map H3. Dorilaíou 6.
Little bar open until sunrise.

Central
Map E4. Plateía Kolonáki 14.
Hottest drinking spot in town.

SHOPPING

Apivita
Map E4. Solonos 26.
Sells natural cosmetics that make great gifts.

Folli Follie
Map E4. Solonos 25.
Affordably priced jewellery, bags and other accessories.

Yeshop
Map E4. Pindarou 38.
Edgy fashion from Greece's best young designers.

OMÓNIA AND
NORTHERN ATHENS

Northern Athens grew up in the early 1800s when King Otto declared Athens the new capital of Greece. It is made up of wide avenues, grand Neo-Classical public buildings and elegant homes and shops. In direct contrast, Omónia is one of Athens' oldest, most well worn districts.

SIGHTS AT A GLANCE

Historic Areas and Buildings
Athens University and
   Academy of Arts **3**
Central Market **5**
Polytechnic **9**

Squares, Parks and Gardens
Pedíou tou Áreos **12**
Plateía Exarcheia **10**
Plateía Omónia **6**
Stréfi Hill **11**

Museums and Galleries
City of Athens Museum **2**
Epigraphical Museum **8**
National Archaeological
   Museum **7**
National Historical Museum **1**
Theatrical Museum **4**

SEE ALSO

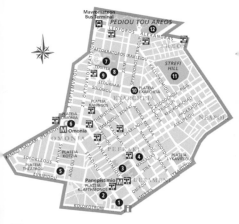

KEY

M Metro

🚏 Trolleybus stop

| 0 metres | | 500 |
| 0 yards | | 500 |

◀ The elegant façade of the Neo-Classical University building

National Historical Museum ❶

Map D4. Stadíou 13. Open Tue–Sun except public hols. Adm charge (free Sun).

Originally home to the first Greek Parliament in 1871, this building opened as the National Historical Museum in 1961. The museum covers all the major events of Greek history from the Byzantine period to the 20th century in a chronological display. The collection also focuses on major parliamentary figures, philhellenes and leaders in the War of Independence.

Upstairs sitting room recreated in the City of Athens Museum

restored in 1980 as a museum devoted to royal memorabilia, furniture and portraits, maps and prints. It offers a look at life during the early years of King Otto's reign. Exhibits include the manuscript of the 1843 constitution and a scale model of the city as it was in 1842. The museum also has a fine art collection.

Athens University and Academy of Arts ❸

Map D3. Panepistimíou.

The city's university and the Academy of Arts are two of the most important Neo-Classical buildings in Athens. The column bases and capitals of the university entrance are replicas of those in the Acropolis Propylaia, and the Academy entrance is based on the eastern side of the Erectheion. The frescoes on the university building depict personifications of the arts around King Otto I, who commissioned the

Neo-Classical façade of the National Historical Museum

City of Athens Museum ❷

Map D4. Paparrigopoúlou 7, Plateía Klafthmónos. Open Wed–Mon except public hols. Adm charge.

King Otto and Queen Amalía lived here from 1831 until their new palace, today's Voulí parliament building in Plateía Syntágmatos (*see p34*), was completed in 1838. It was joined to the next door house to create what was known as the Old Palace. It was

Academy of Arts Statue

rebuilding of the capital in the 1830s. The architects he chose turned to the popular European style of Neo-Classicism and, within 50 years, an elegant modern city had emerged.

Theatrical Museum ④

Map E3. Akadamías 50. Open Sun–Fri except Aug, 17 Nov and public hols. Free.

Housed in the basement of a fine Neo-Classical building, this small museum traces Greek theatrical history from Classical times to the present day. There are displays of original programmes, posters, costumes and designs from productions by influential directors such as Károlos Koun. There is also a colourful puppet theatre. Dressing rooms of famous Greek actresses have been recreated to give an insight into their lives.

Central Market ⑤

Map C3. Athinas, Armodiou, Filopimenos and Aristogitonos Streets. Open Mon–Sat.

The enormous meat, fish and spice markets are a sensory overload, especially the meat one. They shouldn't be missed by any but the most squeamish. Several restaurants and a Greek folk music haunt dot the meat market, serving up the sales of the day until dawn. Outside, the air around the spice stores is filled with the scent of vanilla, saffron and dried mountain thyme.

Plateía Omónia ⑥

Map C3.

When Athens became the capital of newly independent Greece in 1834, King Otto I invited European architects to devise a new urban plan. Originally, Omónia was intended as one of Athens' main squares, along with Sýntagma and Monastiráki. It was ringed by elegant Neo-Classical hotels and cafés, and centred on fountains and palms. Today, it is a chaotic traffic node where six busy roads meet, and two metro lines connect. Renovation for the 2004 Olympics failed to enhance the area. Although several big modern hotels were refurbished, the concrete-surfaced square is still a meeting point for the poor and homeless.

Fish stall in the Central Market

The Neo-Classical entrance to the National Archaeological Museum

National Archaeological Museum ❼

Map D2. 44 Patision. Open daily (times vary). Adm charge.

Opened in 1891, this superb museum brought together a collection that had previously been stored all over the city. New wings were added in 1939. The priceless collection was then dispersed and buried underground during World War II to protect it from possible damage. The museum reopened in 1946 but it took a further 50 years of renovation and reorganization finally to do justice to its formidable collection. With the combination of such unique exhibits as the Mycenaean gold, along with the unrivalled amount of sculpture, pottery and jewellery on display, this is without doubt one of the world's finest museums.

A Cycladic figurine

Exploring the Collection

Displaying its treasures in chronological order, the museum presents an impressive and thorough overview of Greek art through the centuries.

Beginning with early Cycladic figurines and continuing through the Greek Bronze Age, the exhibits end with the glories of Hellenistic period bronzes and a collection of busts of Roman emperors. High points in between include the numerous gold artifacts found at Mycenae, the elegant Archaic *koúroi* statues and the many examples of fine Classical sculpture.

Neolithic and Cycladic Art

The dawning of Greek civilization (3500–2900 BC) saw primitive decorative vases and figures such as the harp-player shown above. This collection also contains terracotta figurines, jewellery and a selection of weapons.

Simple painted Neolithic clay vase

Mycenaean death mask originally thought to be that of Agamemnon

Mycenaean Art

The museum's most popular attraction is the Hall of Mycenaean Antiquities. The Mycenaeans were famed both for their prowess as warriors and their hoards of gold. Parts of those shining hoards are displayed here, including the legendary Mask of Agamemnon.

Geometric and Archaic Art

Famed for its monumental burial vases, the Geometric period developed a more ornate style in the 7th century BC with the introduction of animal, plant and mythological motifs. By the 6th century BC the full artistry of the black-figure vases had developed.

Classical Sculpture

The collection of Classical sculpture contains both fine statues and a selection of grave monuments.

Roman and Hellenistic Sculpture

Although a large number of Greek bronzes were lost in

Youth of Antikýthera

antiquity, as metal was melted down in times of emergency for making weapons, there are some fine pieces on display such as the Youth of Antikýthera, found in the sea.

Other Collections

The museum also houses several smaller collections. Among these is the dazzling Eléni Stathátou collection of jewellery from the Bronze Age to the Byzantine period and the Karapános collection, which contains many fine bronzes. Other displays include the recently opened Egyptian collection and the Bronze collection.

Thíra Frescoes

The highly advanced settlement of Akrotíri, on the island of Thíra (Santoríni) was buried under a volcanic eruption in the 16th century BC. Two of the famous frescoes discovered at Akrotíri on the island in 1967, and originally thought to be from the mythical city of Atlantis, are displayed in the museum.

Pottery Collection

The strength of this vast collection lies not only in its size, but also in the quality of specific works, representing the flowering of Greek ceramic art especially in the 5th century BC.

Epigraphical Museum ❽

Map D2. Tositsa 1. Open Tue–Sun. Free.

Housed here is one of the world's most precious collections of ancient inscriptions, including the official records of early Athens carved on stone and marble slabs. It's a fascinating trove of Athenian lore. The most important exhibits include a decree by the assembly of Athens ordering the evacuation of the city before the Persian invasion in 480 BC and a law concerning temple-worship on the Acropolis.

Polytechnic ❾

Map D2. 28 Oktovriou.

The top educational institution in Greece, Athens Polytechnic, dates from 1836 and occupies these Neo-Classical buildings. On 17 November 1973, the military dictatorship deployed tanks to quash a student uprising here. Over 20 people were killed and the junta fell from power. Since then, Greek law prohibits the police from entering educational buildings and gives students asylum within them. On 17 November each year, politicians place flowers on the memorial.

Statue of the Fallen Student on the walkway near the Polytechnic

Informal cafés in Plateía Exarcheía

Plateía Exarcheía ❿

Map D2. Exarcheia.

In bohemian Exarcheía, Athens' student quarter, the main public meeting place is a triangular piazza, rimmed with informal cafés. The neighbourhood is renowned for anarchist groups and rivalry between students and the police. The alternative crowd flock here for the down-to-earth tavernas, bars and open-air summer cinemas. However, Exarcheía's elegant 19th-century Neo-Classical buildings are gradually being restored, bringing in an air of gentrification.

The far-reaching view of Athens from the top of tree-clad Stréfi Hill

Stréfi Hill ⓫

Map E2. Entrance off Emmanouil Benáki.

The green lung of Exarcheía, rugged Stréfi Hill hosts an informal park, planted with pines, cypresses, eucalyptus, Mediterranean shrubs, cacti and agaves. A maze of paths and steps lead up to the 168-m (550-ft) peak, affording great views over Athens and out to sea. The facilities include a restaurant and *ouzeri*, a basketball court, a children's playground and a small, stone amphitheatre. Stréfi Hill is named after the Stréfi family, who gave the land to Athens City Council in 1963.

A palm offers respite from the heat in the park of Pediou tou Areos

Pediou tou Areos 🕛

Map E1. Leoforos Alexandras.

The largest park in Athens is green and spacious and is a good retreat on hot summer days and the walkway lined with busts of Greece's War of Independence heroes is worth a visit. Despite its size, Pediou tou Areos has the feel of a neighbourhood park, with old ladies sitting on benches and kids riding bikes. Because of its close proximity to political and intellectual Exarcheía, it is often the scene of rallies, outdoor concerts and cultural events such as the annual book fair.

STREET LIFE

RESTAURANTS

Obi
Map D4. Plateía Agíon Theodoron 4 and Skouleniou 2.
Tel 210 331 4330.
Cheap
Informal café-restaurant.

Yiantes
Map E3. Valtetsiou 44.
Tel 210 330 1369.
Cheap
Creative taverna classics.

Alexandreia
Map D1. Metsóvou 13.
Tel 210 821 0004.
Moderate
Middle Eastern food with indoor and outdoor seating.

BARS AND CAFÉS

Karavan
Map E4. Voukourestiou 11.
Sweet treats in a shop alcove.

See p80 for price codes.

Loumidis
Map C4. Aiolou 106.
Vast coffee shop specializing in the traditional Greek/Turkish brew.

Rembetiki Istoria
Map E2. Ippokratous 181.
Greek blues bar.

SHOPPING

Stoa tou Vivliou
Map D3. Between Panepistimiou, Pezmazoglou and Stadiou.
For bowls, platters, vases and ornaments.

Eleftheroudakis
Map D4. Panepistimiou 17.
Seven floors of English and Greek books and a café.

Notos Galleries
Map C3. Aiolou 99.
Department store selling local and international goods.

FURTHER AFIELD

Beyond the sprawl of Athens lies the region of
Attica. Rising up in the north are pine-forested
hills to explore, such as Mount Párnitha, while
all around the coast lie the atmospheric remains
of ancient sites. In contrast to these is the busy
port of Piraeus with its smart shops, fine
architecture and relaxed waterside restaurants.

SIGHTS AT A GLANCE

Ancient Brauron **8**
Ancient Eleusis *pp54–5* **3**
Ancient Oropós **5**
Marathónas **7**
Monastery of Dafní
  pp52–3 **2**
Mount Párnitha **4**

Piraeus **1**
Ramnoús **6**
Soúnio **9**

SEE ALSO

• *Street Life p57*

KEY

✈ Airport
⛴ Ferry port
▬ Motorway
▬ Main road
═ Other road

0 km   10
0 miles   10

◄ *Temple of Poseidon, Cape Soúnio*

Yachts moored in Pasalimáni, which once harboured the Ottoman fleet

Piraeus ❶

10 km (6 miles) SW of Athens, Attica.

One of the biggest Mediterranean ports, Piraeus is also one of the largest cities in Greece. It has been the port of Athens since ancient times. Today, on the streets behind the main ferry port, there are smart restaurants and shops, as well as some fine examples of Neo-Classical architecture, such as the **Town Hall**. South of the railway station lies the lively market area with fruit and vegetable stalls, fishmongers', ships' chandlers and hardware stores. On Sunday mornings there is also a flea market. Piraeus has two harbours. The first harbour, **Pasalimáni**, is filled with

Archaeological Museum bronze

luxurious yachts. Hydrofoils depart from here for the Argo-Saronic islands. **Mikrolímano**, the second port, houses many colourful fishing boats and is popular for its waterside restaurants.

Archaeological Museum

Odos Chariláou Trikoúpi 31. Open Tue–Sun except Aug and public hols. Adm charge.

This is home to some stunning bronzes. Near the museum are the remains of a 2nd-century BC theatre.

Municipal Theatre

Agíou Konstantínou 2. Open Tue–Sun. Free.

This is one of the largest modern theatres in Greece. Today, it is the home of the **Municipal Art Gallery** and the **Museum of Stage Decor**.

Hellenic Maritime Museum

Aktí Themistokléous. Open Tue–Sat (times vary) except public hols. Adm charge.

This museum explores the fascinating world of Greek seafaring. As part of the museum, the old naval ship *Averof*, berthed nearby, is also open to visitors.

Open-air tables overlooking the Mediterranean Sea at Piraeus

Monastery of Dafní ❷

See pp52–3.

Eleusis ❸

See pp54–5.

Mount Párnitha ❹

Attica.

This rugged range extends nearly 25 km (16 miles) from east to west. It provides spectacular alpine views and is rich in fauna, all within an hour's drive of Athens. Birds of prey circle the summit of

The tiny chapel of Agía Triáda on the hillside of Mount Párnitha

Karampóla at 1,413 m (4,635 ft). Wild flowers are abundant, particularly in autumn and spring when cyclamen and crocus carpet the mountain. Still little used by hikers, the mountain has plenty of demanding trails. At the small town of **Acharnés**, a cable car ascends to a casino perched at over 900 m (3,000 ft).

Ancient Oropós ❺

Kálamos, Attica. Open daily except public hols. Adm charge.

The peaceful sanctuary of Oropós is dedicated to Amphiáraos, a hero credited with healing powers. It became a healing centre in the 4th century BC, when its Doric temple and sacrificial altar were built. Houses erected during the Roman period, when the area became a popular spa centre, are still visible along with a long *stoa* where patients were treated. Above them lie the remains of a theatre and opposite the altar is a water clock dating from the 4th century BC.

Ramnoús ❻

Attica. Open daily (Sanctuary of Nemesis only) except public hols. Adm charge.

Ramnoús is home to the only Greek sanctuary dedicated to Nemesis, the goddess of vengeance. Within its compound, two temples are preserved side by side. The smaller Temple of Themis dates from the 6th century BC. The larger Temple of Nemesis, built in the mid-5th century BC in the Doric style, contained a statue of Nemesis.

Remains of the Temple of Nemesis, goddess of vengeance, at Ramnoús

Monastery of Dafní ❷

This 11th-century Byzantine monastery was built on the site of an ancient sanctuary dedicated to Apollo. It was named after the laurels *(dáfnes)* that used to grow here. In the 16th century, Greek Orthodox monks erected the elegant cloisters to the south.

An aerial view of the monastery of Dafni complex with the Gothic arcade facing.

The Gothic arcade was built almost 30 years after the main church.

The cloisters were built in the 16th century. On the other side of the courtyard, above a similar arcade, are the monks' cells.

Entrance

The brilliant mosaics *include depictions of the Last Supper and the Washing of the Feet. The finest is the Betrayal by Judas. Christ stands unmoved as Judas kisses him.*

The dome *is 8 m (26 ft) in diameter and 16 m (52 ft) high at the centre.*

The symmetry *of the design makes Dafni one of the most attractive examples of Byzantine architecture in Attica.*

The windows *are surrounded by elaborate three-tiered brickwork.*

Ticket office and museum

VISITORS' CHECKLIST

10 km (6 miles) NW of Athens, Attica. Tel 210 581 1558. *Being restored – phone for opening details.*

Ancient Eleusis ❸

For 1,400 years, Eleusis was the centre of a religious cult that culminated in the annual Eleusinian Mysteries festival (*see below*). Existing from Mycenaean times, Eleusis was closed by the Romans in AD 392 and was abandoned when the Goths invaded in 396.

The Temple of Telesterion *was built in the 5th century BC. This great hall could hold several thousand people.*

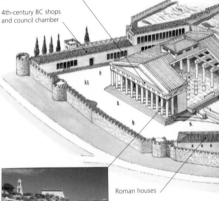

4th-century BC shops and council chamber

Roman houses

Anaktoron *means "palace" and this edifice existed long before the Telesterion, which was built around it. It had a single entrance and was considered to be the holiest part of the site.*

THE ELEUSINIAN MYSTERIES

The rites centred on the myth of the grieving goddess Demeter, who lost her daughter, Persephone, to Hades for nine months a year. The only initial requirement for a *mystes* (or initiate) was to be neither a murderer nor a barbarian. Not much is known about their rites and beliefs as *mystai* were sworn to secrecy.

The Ploutonion *was a sanctuary to Hades, god of the Underworld and abductor of Persephone. This cave is said to be where Persephone was returned to Earth.*

The Greater Propylaia *was the entrance to the sanctuary of Demeter and was built from marble in the 2nd century AD.*

Temple of Artemis Propylaia

This reconstruction *is of Ancient Eleusis as it was in Roman times around AD 150.*

The Lesser Propylaia *was the second gate into the sanctuary of Demeter. This fragment shows sheaves of grain and poppies, which were used to make kykeon, the drink of the initiates.*

VISITORS' CHECKLIST

Gioka 2, Eleusis, 22 km (14 miles) NW of Athens. Tel 210 554 6019. Open Tue–Sun except public hols. Adm charge.

Marathónas ❼

Attica. **Site and Museum**
Open Tue–Sun except public
hols. Adm charge.

The Marathon Plain is
the site of the great
Battle of Marathon,
where the Athenians
defeated the Persians.
The burial mound of
the Athenians lies
4 km (2 miles) from
the modern town of
Marathónas. Marked
by a simple *stele* of
a fallen warrior, it
contains the ashes
of the 192 Athenian
warriors who died
in the battle. The
burial mound of
the Plataians and
royal Mycenaean
tombs are nearby
in the village of Vraná.
The Plataians were the
only other Greeks who sent
warriors in time to assist the
Athenians already at the
battle. The museum displays
finds from these local sites.

*Monument at the site of
the Battle of Marathon*

Ancient Brauron ❽

10 km (6 miles) NE of
Markópoulo, Attica.

Brauron is one of the most
evocative sites near Athens.
Although little remains of its
former architectural glory,
finds in the museum reveal

*Remains of the Parthenon of the
Bear Maidens at Brauron*

its importance as the
centre of worship of
Artemis, goddess of
childbirth and
protectress of animals.
The centre of the site
lies just north of the
prehistoric acropolis.
The 5th-century BC
Doric Temple of
Artemis, of which only
the foundations
remain, formed the
focal point of the
sanctuary. From here a
path leads to the oldest
cult site in the
sanctuary, said to
be the Tomb of
Iphigénia, the
high priestess of
Artemis. Next to
the site are the
foundations of the
Sacred House,
which was used as a home
by the cult's priestesses. The
most extensive remains are
at the Parthenon of the Bear
Maidens where girls may
have performed a dance
disguised as bears. This
courtyard is surrounded by
a late 5th-century BC *stoa*.

Soúnio ❾

9 km (6 miles) SW of Lávrio,
Attica. Open daily. Adm charge.

The temple of Poseidon,
built on a site set back from
sheer cliffs tumbling into the
Aegean Sea at Soúnio (Cape
Sounion), was ideally
located for worship of the
powerful god of the sea.
Its brilliant white marble
columns have been a
landmark for ancient and
modern mariners alike.
The present temple, built in
444 BC, stands on the site of

The ruins of the Temple of Poseidon at Soúnio

older ruins. An Ionic marble frieze is located on the east side of the temple's main approach path. It is very eroded, but is known to have depicted scenes from the mythological battle of the Lapiths and centaurs, and also the adventures of the hero Theseus, who was thought to be the son of Poseidon, according to some legends. Local marble, taken from quarries at nearby Agriléza, was used for the temple's 34 slender Doric columns, of which 15 survive today.

STREET LIFE

RESTAURANTS

Achinos
Akri Themistokléous 51, Piraeus. Tel 210 452 6944.
Moderate
Creative mezes with sea views.

Jimmy & the Fish
Akti Koumoundourou 46, Piraeus. Tel 210 412 4417.
Expensive
Fine seafood and service in excellent location by harbour.

Pappas
Thesalonikis 2, Thrakomakedones, Párnitha. Tel 210 243 1232.
Cheap
Traditional taverna set in the foothills of Mount Párnitha.

Psaropoula–Bibikos
Avlakiou 118, Porto Rafti. Tel 229 907 1292.
Moderate
Provides a tasty lunch after touring the ruins at Brauron.

Syrtaki
2km (1 m) N of Poseidon Temple, Soúnio.
Tel 229 203 9125.
Cheap
Traditional menu in a non-touristy taverna with a shaded terrace overlooking the sea.

BARS AND CAFÉS

Café Freddo
Plateía Alexandras 1, Piraeus.
Serves morning coffee, ice creams, pre-dinner cocktails and nightcaps.

Don Kihotis
Vasileos Pavlou 68, Kastella, near Piraeus.
Roof terrace with dreamy, romantic views.

Wild Thing
Akti Dilaveri 16, Mikrolimano.
The first in a row of super-trendy late night café-bars.

See p80 for price codes.

DAY TRIPS FROM ATHENS

The part of Greece that stretches out to the west of Athens is rich in history and the landscape has remained the same for millennia. This is a fascinating area to explore and is home to some of the most incredible sights in the world such as the Corinth Canal and the theatre at Epidaurus.

SIGHTS AT A GLANCE

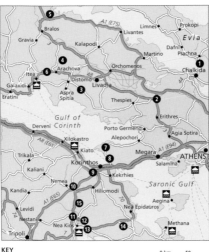

KEY

⛴ Ferry port

▬ Motorway

▬ Main road

═ Other road

| 0 km | 50 |
| 0 miles | 50 |

◀ *Náfplio, seen from the stairs leading to the town's Venetian citadel.*

Evvoia ❶

Chalkída: 78 km (49 miles) from Athens.

After Crete, Evvoia is Greece's largest island. It is largely unspoilt and easily accessible via a bridge from the mainland. Its varied history and landscape make it a microcosm of the whole country. From Macedonian rule in 338 BC until Turkish dominion ended in 1833, the island suffered at the hands of occupying forces including Roman, Frankish and Venetian.

Northern Evvoia consists of forests, rivers, beaches and hot springs. Separated by the central mountains, the south is rough and dusty with sheep grazing in flinty fields and roads snaking along cliff tops.

15th-century mosque in Chalkída

The capital of the island is **Chalkída**, a modern town with a mixed populace of Muslims, Jews and Orthodox Greeks. Although much of Chalkída is dominated by commercial activity, there are two areas of the town that are worth a visit: the waterfront, which overlooks the Evripos channel with its bustling enclosed market, and the old Kástro quarter. In this quarter's deserted streets, many houses still bear the traces of their

Sarcophagus detail outside the Thebes Archaeological Museum

Venetian and Turkish ancestry, with timbered façades or marble heraldic carving. It also has an imposing variety of religious buildings including a 19th-century synagogue and a 15th-century mosque.

Thebes ❷

97 km (58 miles) from Athens. **Archaeological Museum** Plateía Threpsiádou 1. Open daily (times vary). Adm charge.

Although it was a briefly the most powerful city in Greece in the 4th century BC, the Thebes of today is more of a quiet provincial town. Thebes' original acropolis has been built over, but excavations have unearthed Mycenaean walls as well as jewellery, pottery and important tablets, now in the Archaeological Museum. The museum's courtyard and well-tended garden stand alongside a 13th-century Frankish tower. Eastwards from the museum, a bridge marks the site of the Fountain of Oedipus where the legendary King Oedipus is said to have washed blood from his hands after unwittingly killing his father on his way to the city.

Osios Loúkas ❸

See pp62–3.

Fir-covered foothills beneath the ridge of Mount Parnassus

Mount Parnassus **4**

184 km (114 miles) from Athens.

Rising to a height of 2,457 m (8,060 ft), the limestone mass of Mount Parnassus dominates the eastern region of Stereá Elláda. Vultures and golden eagles are common, as are wolves, which come down from the mountains in winter. The village of **Aráchova** is the best base for exploring the area and is renowned for its wine, cheese and sheepskin rugs. There are many mountain trails for summer hikes but a good map is recommended.

From Aráchova, the ski centre at **Fterólaka** is only 26 km (16 miles) away. It is open from December to April. In summer, Fterólaka functions as an excursion centre.

Thermopylae **5**

188 km (117 miles) from Athens.

A short drive east of the Greek town of Lamía, the Athens road crosses the Pass of Thermopylae. It was here, in 480 BC, that an army of some 7,000 soldiers, under Leonidas I of Sparta's command, met an over-whelming force from Persia. According to the Greek historian Herodotus, the Persian army numbered 2,641,610. Though Leonidas held the pass for a number of days, the Persians forced a path through and attacked the Greeks from the rear. Only two Greek soldiers survived the ordeal, after which all of central Greece, including Athens, fell to the Persians. The Persian land forces were eventually defeated at the Battle of Plataiai in 479 BC.

A bronze statue of King Leonidas, cast in 1955, stands at the side of the road opposite the burial mound of the soldiers who died here. To the left of the mound are the famous sulphur springs from which Thermopylae was given its name, which means the "Hot Gates".

Bronze statue of King Leonidas at the Pass of Thermopylae

Osios Loúkas ❸

This monastery was built around 1011 and dedicated to a local hermit called Holy Luke. The octagonal style of the main church became a hallmark of late Byzantine church design while the mosaics inside lifted Byzantine art into its final great period.

The monastery, *seen from the west, with the slopes of Mount Elikónas in the background.*

The Theotókos, *built in the early 11th century, is a smaller church dedicated to the Mother of God.*

North transept

The monastic cells *are small with arched roofs.*

The exterior *is a mixture of dressed Póros stone and red brick.*

Western entrance hall

The Washing of the Apostles' Feet *is based on a style dating to the 6th century. This 11th-century work is the finest of the mosaics. Set on a gold background, it depicts Christ teaching his apostles humility.*

The dome is decorated with an imposing 16th-century mural of Christ surrounded by saints and angels.

The apse has a mosaic of the Virgin and Child pre-dating a devastating earthquake in 1659.

The crypt contains the sarcophagus of Holy Luke and such frescoes as this Descent from the Cross.

The refectory was used as a workshop as well as for meals. It now contains a museum of Byzantine sculpture.

The southwest chapel has early-11th-century frescoes.

VISITORS' CHECKLIST

8 km (5 miles) E of Distomo. Tel 22670 22797. Open daily (times vary). Adm charge.

Dramatic view over the Theatre at Delphi, which was built 2,500 years ago

Ancient Delphi ⑥

Mount Parnassus. **Site and Museum** Open daily (times vary) except public hols. Adm charge.

According to legend, when Zeus released two eagles from opposite ends of the world their paths crossed in the sky above Delphi, establishing the site as the centre of the Earth. From the end of the 8th century BC, individuals from all over the ancient world visited Delphi. They believed it to be a dwelling place of Apollo and they came to consult the god on what course of action to take. The Delphic Oracle was the means through which worshippers could hear the words of the god Apollo, spoken through a priestess. The oracle was abolished in AD 393 when the Byzantine Empire became Christian.

Theatre

The theatre, built in the 4th century BC, seats 5,000 people. It rivals Epidaurus (*see p71*) as one of the finest theatres in Greece.

Marmaria Precinct

The Marmaria Precinct is where the Sanctuary of Athena Pronaia can be found. At the sanctuary's entrance stand the ruins of a 4th-century BC temple dedicated to Athena. At the far end of the sanctuary are the remains of an earlier temple to the goddess, which was built around 510 BC. Between the two temples stands the circular *tholos*, which was originally surrounded by 20 columns. The purpose of this structure is still unknown.

The tholos beside the Sanctuary of Athena Pronaia, Marmaria Precinct

Stadium

This is one of the best preserved stadia in the country. Almost 200 m (655 ft) long, the stadium held 7,000 spectators, who gathered for the field and track events every four years during the Pythian Games. These, after the Olympic games, were the most important sporting event in the Greek calendar. Each winner was awarded a laurel wreath and the right to have his statue in the sanctuary. The games grew out of a musical festival, held every eight years, to celebrate Apollo's mythical slaying of the serpent Python. From 582 BC athletic events in the stadium were added and the festival became known as the Pythian Games. The present structure dates from Roman times.

Castalian Spring

Before entering the Sacred Precinct, it is believed that everyone visiting Delphi for religious purposes had to purify themselves in the waters of the Castalian Spring. A number of niches in the rock once held the votive offerings left for the nymph Castalia, to whom the spring was dedicated.

The niches of the Castalian Spring, where visitors were purified

The Stadium at Delphi

Gymnasium

Water from the spring ran down to this area to provide cold baths for the athletes. East of the baths lies the training area, surrounded by the remains of the changing rooms and training quarters. As well as an outdoor running track, a covered track provided a venue for the games in bad weather. Delphi's philosophers and poets also taught here.

Delphi Museum

The museum at Delphi contains a collection of sculptures and architectural remains of an importance second only to those of the Athenian Acropolis *(see pp10–11)*. The most famous of the museum's exhibits is a life-size bronze statue, the *Charioteer*. The statue was made to commemorate a chariot victory in the Pythian Games in 478 BC. Don't miss the Omphalos stone. This is a Hellenistic or Roman copy of the stone that was believed to have marked the place above which Zeus's eagles met, establishing the sanctuary of Delphi as the centre of the Earth.

Perahora ❼

13 km (8 miles) W of Loutráki,
Peloponnese.

Perahora, or the "Land
Beyond" as it was called by
the ancient Corinthians, is a
pine-clad promontory jutting
into the Gulf of Corinth. On
it lie the ruins of the ancient
city of Perahora and the
Heraion – a sanctuary to the
goddess Hera, probably
founded during the 8th
century BC. Not much
remains of the temple but
the site has an incomparable
setting above a tiny cove.
Nearby, scenic Lake
Vouliagméni, 3 km (2 miles)
east, is fringed by pines,
with the best swimming
and a selection of tavernas
at its west end.

Loutráki ❽

84 km (53 miles) W of Athens,
Peloponnese.

Overlooking a long narrow
pebble beach, Loutráki
developed into a spa resort

Waterfall at Loutráki

in 1847, when visitors began
coming here to drink the
local mineral waters to
soothe digestive
disturbances, and to bathe in
the thermal springs as a cure
for a wide variety of diseases
and complaints. The name
Loutráki is derived from
loutra, meaning "hot
springs". Greece's oldest
casino opened here in 1930.
It was renovated in 1995 to
make it one of Europe's
biggest 24-hour casinos.
Today, it is a popular
Athenian weekend
destination, with some 60
hotels, several spas, a casino
and water sports facilities.

Corinth ❾

See pp68–9.

Ancient Neméa ❿

5 km (3 miles) NE of Neméa,
Peloponnese. Open daily (times
vary) except public hols.
Adm charge.

Evocatively occupying an
isolated rural valley, the site
of Ancient Neméa is a local
landmark, with the Doric
columns of its 4th-century
BC Zeus temple plainly
visible from afar. At the west
end of the temple, a deep
underground crypt has been
exposed. To the southwest,
a Hellenistic bathhouse is
being excavated; so far only
the plunge-pool and feed
system have been revealed.
Recent digs have uncovered
a Byzantine village, which
took root here in the 4th
century AD, including
graves, kilns, a basilica and a
baptistry. The museum has
interesting reconstructions

Three Doric columns of the Temple of Zeus, Ancient Neméa

and old engravings. The Hellenistic stadium, 400 m (1,300 ft) to the southeast, has the earliest known vaulted entrance tunnel.

Argos ⓫

140 km (86 miles) SW of Athens, Peloponnese.

Although one of the oldest settlements in Greece, modern Argos is a busy market town, with its open-air fairground next to a restored Neo-Classical marketplace. To the east of the central square, the Archaeological Museum exhibits local finds from all eras. Highlights include a bronze breastplate and helmet, and an Archaic pottery fragment showing Odysseus blinding Polyphimos. The most visible traces of Ancient Argos lie on the way to Trípoli (southwest), where Roman baths and an amphitheatre are dwarfed by the size of one of the largest

and most steeply raked theatres in the Greek world. From here, a path climbs Lárisa hill, one of Argos's two ancient acropoleis.

Tiryns ⓬

4 km (2 miles) NW of Náfplio, Peloponnese. Open daily. Adm charge.

The 13th-century BC citadel of Tiryns confirms Homer's epithet "mighty-walled". A 700-m (2,300-ft) circuit of walls reaches a thickness of 8 m (26 ft). The fortifications, over double their present height, were necessarily stronger than those of Mycenae (*see pp72–3*) as Tiryns was not on a naturally strong site. The bluff on which it stood was only 18 m (59 ft) higher than the surrounding plain which, in ancient times, was a salt marsh. The lower acropolis was the last part to be enclosed and was used to protect commoners, animals and a water supply.

Excavated ruins of the mighty-walled Tiryns

Corinth 9

Ancient Corinth

7 km (4 miles) SW of modern Corinth, Peloponnese. **Site and Museum** Open daily (times vary) except public hols. Adm charge.

Ancient Corinth derived its prosperity from its position on a narrow isthmus between the Corinthian and Saronic gulfs. Transporting goods across this isthmus, even before the canal was built, provided the shortest route from the eastern Mediterranean to the Adriatic and Italy. Founded in Neolithic times, the town was razed in 146 BC by the Romans, who rebuilt it a century later. Attaining a population of 750,000, Ancient Corinth gained a reputation for licentious living, which St Paul attacked when he came here in AD 52. Excavations have revealed the vast extent of the city that was destroyed by earthquakes in Byzantine times. The ruins constitute the largest Roman township in Greece.

Marble-paved road linking Ancient Corinth to the port of Lechaion

Doric columns of the Temple of Apollo at Ancient Corinth

Temple of Apollo

The most striking structure of the lower city is the Temple of Apollo. It was one of the few buildings preserved by the Romans when they rebuilt the site in 46 BC. At the southeast corner of the temple, an ingenious stepped ramp leads to the temple terrace.

Acrocorinth

4 km (2 miles) S of Ancient Corinth. Open daily. Free.

Acrocorinth has been held and refortified by every occupying power in Greece since Roman times. Entry to this fortress above the main site is on the west, where the natural defences are weakest, through three successive gateways from different eras. Beyond sprawls a 24-ha (60-acre) terraced wilderness of minaret stumps, Muslim tombs and lonely mosques or chapels – all that remains of a town that was abandoned almost 200 years ago when its last defenders, the Turks, were defeated. The lower elevation at the southwest corner of the 5-km (3-mile) circuit of walls sports a Venetian tower, while the true, northeast summit bears the scant

The entrance to Acrocorinth, with its three gateways

foundations of an Aphrodite temple, attended in antiquity by 1,000 sacred prostitutes. It was against such practices that St Paul wrote his "letters to the Corinthians". Today its attraction is one of the most sweeping views in the whole of Greece, up to 60 km (37 miles) in all directions.

Museum

Open daily. Adm charge.
The site museum ranks among Greece's best provincial collections. All periods of the ancient town's history are represented, though the Roman gallery in the west wing is particularly rich. Here pride of place goes to 2nd-century AD mosaics lifted from the floors of nearby villas. Also in the west wing are some of the 274 objects stolen from the museum in 1990 and recovered nine years later in Miami. The east gallery features older artifacts such as rare Attic ware from the 5th century BC and 7th- and 6th-century BC pottery, some painted with typical Corinthian fantastic beasts. At the shrine of Asklepios,

Mosaic of Bacchus

just within the northern boundary of the ancient city, votive offerings in the shape of afflicted body parts were found and are on display. Stone reliefs in the central courtyard include depictions of the Labours of Herakles.

Corinth Canal

Peloponnese.
Stormy cape Matapan, or Taínaro, the southernmost point of the Peloponnese, was one of the dreaded capes of antiquity. Rather than risk sailing around it, boats would be unloaded on one shore of this isthmus, dragged along the 6 km (4 miles) paved slipway and then refloated the other side. The traffic enriched Corinth and inspired plans for a canal. Emperor Nero began building it, but the project was only completed between 1882 and 1893. The 23-m (75-ft) wide canal is obsolete in an age of giant container ships that easily weather the cape, but small freighters squeezing through are regularly seen from the road bridge above.

A ship being guided by a tugboat through the narrow Corinth Canal

The rooftops of Náfplio

Náfplio ⓭

Peloponnese.

With its marble pavements, looming castles and homogenous architecture, Náfplio is the most elegant town in mainland Greece. It emerged from obscurity in the 13th century and endured many sieges during the struggles between Venice and Turkey for the Peloponnesian ports. From 1829 until 1834, the town was the first capital of liberated Greece.

Exploring Náfplio

Náfplio occupies the northern side of a peninsula at the head of the Argolic Gulf. Since the Venetian period, Plateía Syntágmatos has been the hub of public life. The two mosques in the square were built by the victorious Ottomans. One is now a cinema and the other one was where the Greek parliament first met. The cathedral, Agios Geórgios, was built as a mosque during the first Ottoman occupation (1540–1686). The Catholic church is also a converted mosque and contains a monument honouring fallen philhellenes.

Archaeological Museum

Plateía Syntágmatos. Open daily (times vary). Adm charge.
Exhibits largely centre on Mycenaean artifacts from local sites, including Tiryns.

Folk Art Museum

Vas. Alexandrou 1. Open daily (times vary). Adm charge.
This museum, established by the Peloponnesian Folklore Foundation, is mostly devoted to textiles.

Akronafplía

W of Palamídi. Unrestricted access.
Akronafplía was the site of the Byzantine and early medieval town and contains four Venetian castles.

Palamídi

Polyzoïdou. Open daily (times vary) except public hols. Adm charge.
This huge 18th-century Venetian citadel consists of a single curtain wall enclosing seven self-sufficient forts. It is the largest complex of its kind in Greece.

Boúrtzi

NW of harbour.
This island fortress defended the only navigable passage in the bay; the channel could be closed off by a chain extending from the fortress to the town.

The fortified isle of Boúrtzi, which defends the navigation channel

Looking down at the stage at the Theatre of Epidaurus

Epidaurus ⑭

30 km (19 miles) E of Náfplio, Peloponnese. **Site and Museum** Open daily (times vary) except public hols. Adm charge.

Though most renowned for its magnificent theatre, the Sanctuary of Epidaurus was an extensive therapeutic and religious centre, dedicated to the healing god Asklepios. A mortal physician deified by Zeus after his death for retrieving a patient from the underworld, Asklepios was depicted in his temple here clutching a staff and flanked by a dog and a serpent – common symbols of natural wisdom. This sanctuary was active from the 6th century BC until at least the 2nd century AD.

Theatre

Designed by Polykleitos the Younger late in the 4th century BC, the theatre is well known for its near-perfect acoustics. It has the only circular stage to have survived from antiquity, though the altar that once stood in the centre has now gone. Today, the theatre is the venue for a summer festival of ancient drama.

Asklepieion

Outside the theatre is the sprawling Asklepieion – the ancient spa and resort devoted to Asklepios. On the northern edge of this sanctuary lies the monumental gateway, which was the original entrance. Also preserved are the partial remains of the Sacred Way that led from the gateway to the coastal town of ancient Epidaurus. At the northwestern end of the sanctuary stand the remains of the *tholos* (a circular building of uncertain function) and to the north of this lies a hall where patients slept. Here they would await a diagnostic dream or a visit from harmless serpents. Only the foundations of Asklepios' temple have survived, lying to the east of the *tholos*.

Another undisturbed point is the late Classical stadium south of the *tholos*. This was used during the festival in honour of Asklepios.

Burial site at Mycenae that contained six royal family graves

Mycenae ⓰

2 km (1 mile) N of Mykínes,
Peloponnese. **Site and Museum**
Open daily (times vary) except
public hols. Adm charge.

Legend and history combine
alluringly at Mycenae. The
ancient Greek poet Homer
wrote about the citadel of
"well-built Mycenae, rich
in gold" commanded by
Agamemnon, Greece's most
powerful king during the
Trojan War. And history
confirms that indeed there
was a Trojan War and a
powerful civilization based
in Mycenae.

The fortified palace
complex was uncovered by
the German archaeologist
Heinrich Schliemann in 1874
and is one of the earliest
examples of sophisticated
citadel architecture. The
term "Mycenaean", more
properly late Bronze Age,
applies to an entire culture
spanning the years 1700 to
1100 BC. Only the ruling
class inhabited this hilltop
palace, with artisans and
merchants living just outside
the city walls. It was
abandoned in 1100 BC after
a period of great disruption
in the area.

Tombs of Mycenae

Unlike their other Greek
contemporaries who would
cremate their dead, the
Mycenaeans buried their
deceased in tombs. Nobles
were entombed in shaft
graves or, later, in *tholos*
("beehive") tombs. These
tombs, found outside the
palace walls, were built
using successive circles of
masonry, each level nudged
steadily inward to narrow
the diameter until the top
could be closed with a single
stone. The entire structure
was then buried, save for an
entrance approached by an
open-air corridor.

*The entrance to the Treasury of
Atreus, with a gap over its lintel*

Treasury of Atreus

The Treasury of Atreus is the most outstanding of the *tholos* tombs. In the Treasury, a Mycenaean king was buried with his weapons and enough food and drink for his journey through the Underworld.

The Treasury is situated at the southern end of the site and dates from the 14th century BC. It is one of only two double-chambered tombs in Greece. It has a 36-m (120-ft) open-air corridor flanked by dressed stone and a small ossuary (the second chamber) that held the bones from previous burials. A 9-m (30-ft) long lintel stone stands over the entrance, weighing almost 120 tonnes (264,550 lb). It is still not known how it was hoisted into place, and is a tribute to Mycenaean building skills.

Noted archaeologist Heinrich Schliemann

The treasury is also known as the Tomb of Agamemnon. However, the legendary Greek king could not have been buried here, as the construction of the tomb predates the estimated period of the Trojan War by more than 100 years.

Tomb of Klytemnestra

Of the other *tholos* tombs only the so-called Tomb of Klytemnestra, which is situated just west of the Lion Gate, is as well preserved as that of the Treasury of Atreus. It is a small, single-chambered sepulchre with narrower and more steeply inclined walls. The finely masoned open-air corridor and similar triangular air hole over the entrance (which also relieved pressure on the lintel) date it back to the same period.

Heinrich Schliemann

Born in Mecklenburg, Germany, Heinrich Schliemann (1822–90) was self-educated and by the age of 47 had become a millionaire, expressly to fund his archaeological digs. Having discovered Troy and demonstrated the factual basis of Homer's epics, he came to Mycenae in 1874 and commenced digging. On discovering a gold death mask that had preserved the skin of a royal skull, he proclaimed: "I have gazed upon the face of Agamemnon!" However, archaeologists have since dated the mask to 300 years earlier than any historical Trojan warrior.

The Lion Gate takes its name from the lions carved above the lintel

Getting Around

There are a variety of transport options to choose from in Athens including the Athens Metro, an extensive bus network and a plentiful supply of taxis. However, the best way to get around is probably on foot as the roads can be very congested.

Athens Metro

The metro, which has three lines, is a fast and reliable means of transport in Athens. One ticket allows travel on any of the three lines and is valid for 90 minutes in one direction. Tickets can be bought at any metro station and must be validated before entering the train – use the machines at the entrances to all platforms. Trains run every 5 minutes from roughly 5am to 12:30am.

Bus Networks

The colour-coded bus network is extensive and bus tickets are cheap. Blue, yellow and white buses cover a network of over 300 routes in Athens. They run daily from 5am to 12.30am and there is also a limited night service. Tickets can be bought individually or in a book of ten, but either way, they must be purchased in advance from a street kiosk, a transport booth or anywhere with the brown, red and white logo, with the words *eisitíria edó*. These tickets can be used on buses (and trolleybuses), and must be stamped in a ticket machine to validate them on boarding.

Trolleybuses

Trolleybuses are purple and yellow in colour and there are over 20 routes that crisscross the city. They provide a good and inexpensive way to get around the central sights. All routes pass the Pláka area. Use the same tickets as for blue, yellow and white buses, and validate them on boarding.

Purple and yellow Athens trolleybus

Walking in Athens

Almost all the museums and major sites are to be found within about a 25-minute walk of Plateía Syntágmatos (*see p34*), which is generally regarded as the city's centre. Athens' roads are often busy, so travelling around on foot is likely to be a quicker option. Always be vigilant when walking, especially at night.

One of Athens' many yellow taxis

Athenian Taxis

Athens' taxis are yellow, cheap and plentiful, but getting one to stop can be difficult especially between 2pm and 3pm when taxi drivers usually change shifts. They can be ordered by phone for a small surcharge or waved down in the street. To hail a taxi, stand on the edge of the pavement and shout out your destination to any cab that slows down. It is common practice for drivers to pick up extra passengers who are heading in your direction. Higher tariffs come into effect between midnight and 5am, and you also pay extra for airport trips and luggage.

Travelling by Funicular

One of the best places for watching the sunset over Athens is the summit of Lykavittós Hill (*see p39*).

Funicular up Lykavittós Hill

You can walk up or take the funicular from Aristíppou. It runs every 20 minutes from 9am to 3am.

Moped Hire

A speedy and fun way to zip around is by moped. If you have a valid driving licence, you can rent one from Moto Rent in the Koukáki area of Athens.

Driving in Athens

Driving in Athens can be a nerve-racking experience. Many streets in the centre are pedestrianized and there are also plenty of one-way streets. The roads are congested, parking spaces are hard to find and drivers are actively discouraged from taking their cars into the city centre by an "odd-even" number plate system.

TRAVEL INFORMATION

For information about fares, routes and timings of the various transport services, go to the Athens Urban Transport Organization website **www.oasa.gr**

Taxis
Athina 1
Tel 210 921 7942.
Ermis
Tel 210 411 5200.

Moped Hire
Moto Rent
Tel 210 923 4939.

Car Hire
Avis
Tel 210 322 4951.
Budget
Tel 210 921 4771.

Survival Guide

Athens is a busy, modern metropolitan centre and it does pay to know something about the nuts and bolts of Greek life when travelling around it. The following information will help you make sense of some of the everyday aspects of life in Athens, and what to do and where to go in an emergency.

MONEY

Currency

Greece uses the common European currency of euros and cents. There are 100 cents to a euro. Notes come in €5, €10, €20, €50 and €100 denominations. Coins come in 1c, 5c, 10c, 20c, 50c, €1 and €2 pieces.

Banks and Exchange Facilities

Banks are normally open from 8am to 2pm Monday to Thursday, and from 8am to 1:30pm on Friday. ATM cash machines are in operation 24 hours a day. Foreign currency exchange is also available at travel agents, post offices, hotels, car-hire agencies and tourist offices.

Standard yellow postbox

Credit and Debit Cards

Credit and debit cards can be used for drawing local currency at cash machines. Visa, MasterCard, American Express and Diners Club are the most widely accepted credit cards in Greece. Credit cards are accepted in larger hotels, restaurants and shops, but you will find that less touristy businesses, such as local tavernas or small shops, accept cash only.

COMMUNICATIONS

Telephones

To use a public telephone, you will need a phone card. If you have difficulty contacting a number, call the Operator (151) or International Operator (139). In an emergency, dial 100 (police), 166 (ambulance) or 199 (fire). The code for Athens is 210. To call abroad from Athens, dial 00, the country code, the local area code (omit the 0) and the number itself.

Postal Services

Greek post offices are usually open from 7:30am to 2pm Monday to Friday. Those with an "Exchange" sign will also change money. Post boxes are yellow and stamps can be bought at post offices and postal agencies.

Internet Cafés

Cafés with web access are springing up all over the city. The best Internet cafés

An Internet café in Athens

in the central area are the Museum Internet Café at Patision 46, Cafe4u at Ippokratous 44, and Bits and Bytes at Akadimias 78. In Piraeus, try Netmania at Vasileos Pavlou 135.

HEALTH AND SECURITY

Emergency medical care in Greece is free for all EU citizens. The European Health Insurance Card covers emergencies only; private medical insurance is needed for all other types of treatment.

Travel Insurance

Public health facilities are limited in Greece and private clinics are expensive. It is advisable to take out comprehensive travel insurance.

Pharmacies

Greek pharmacists are highly qualified and can not only advise on minor ailments, but also dispense medication not usually available over the counter back home. Their premises, *farmakeía*, are identified by a red or green cross on a white background. Pharmacies are open from 8:30am to 2pm but are closed in the afternoon and on Saturday mornings. Details of opening times are posted up in most pharmacy windows.

Personal Safety

The crime rate in Greece is very low compared with other European countries. If you have anything stolen, contact the tourist police.

Police

There are three forces: the regular police, port police and tourist police. Should you suffer a theft, lose your passport or have cause to complain about anything, your case should first be made to the tourist police. Their offices also offer maps, brochures and advice on finding accommodation.

Emergency Services

In case of emergencies the appropriate services to call are listed in the directory below. For accidents or medical emergencies, a 24-hour ambulance service operates in Athens.

Ambulance with the emergency number on its side

DIRECTORY

Ambulance
Tel 166.

Police
Tel 100.

Fire Brigade
Tel 199.

Road Assistance
Tel 104.

Tourist Police
Tel 171.

Doctors
Tel 1016 (2pm–7am).

Hospitals, Clinics and Pharmacies on Duty
Tel 1434.

Poison Treatment Centre
Tel 210 779 3777.

Index